# 5 Steps to Teaching AP Psychology

TEACHER'S MANUAL

## Laura Sheckell, MA

AP Psychology Teacher at Wylie E. Groves High School,
Beverly Hills, Michigan

*Thanks to Greg Jacobs, an AP physics teacher at Woodberry Forest School in Virginia, for developing the 5-step approach used in this teaching guide. Thanks also to Courtney Mayer, an AP environmental science teacher, for creating a sample teacher's manual that AP teachers could use to create their own guide.*

# Introduction to the Teacher's Manual

Nowadays, teachers have no shortage of resources for the AP psychology class. No longer limited to just the teacher and the textbook, today's teachers can utilize online simulations, apps, computer-based homework, video lectures, etc. Even the College Board itself provides so much material related to the AP Psychology exam that the typical teacher—and student—can easily become overwhelmed by an excess of teaching materials and resources.

One vital resource for you and your class is this book. It explains in straight-forward language exactly what a student needs to know for the AP Psychology exam. It also provides a complete review for the test including explanatory materials, questions to check student understanding, and test-like practice exams.

This teacher's manual will take you through the 5 steps of teaching AP psychology. These 5 steps are:

1. **Prepare a strategic plan for the course**

2. **Hold an interesting class every day**

3. **Evaluate your students' progress**

4. **Get students ready to take the AP exam**

5. **Become a better teacher every year**

I'll discuss each of these steps, providing suggestions and ideas of things that I use in my class. I present them here because, over the years, I found that they work. You may have developed a different course strategy, teaching activities, and evaluation techniques. That's great; different things work for different teachers. But I hope you find in this teacher's manual something that will be useful to you.

## STEP 1

# Prepare a Strategic Plan for the Course

The Course and Exam Description (CED) from the College Board, which can be found at: https://apcentral.collegeboard.org/pdf/ap-psychology-course-and-exam-description.pdf?course=ap-psychology, lays out a suggested scope and sequence for the AP psychology class. My suggestion is to stick with the suggested scope and sequence for your first few years. The College Board has set it up in a way that topics and skills build as the year goes on.

But after you have taught the course a few times and feel comfortable with the material, you may want to move topics and units around to better meet your classroom needs. Some

years I have decided to start with Unit 9, Social Psychology, before moving on to Unit 1, Scientific Foundations of Psychology, because Unit 9 is something students enjoyed and got them hooked on psychology. I do like to save Units 6, 7, and 8 (Development; Motivation, Emotion, and Personality; and Clinical Psychology) for the second term as these topics cover material that build on earlier units and also cover the bulk of the exam. Leaving these topics until the spring semester will ensure that students are ready for the advanced skills found in these units and covering these topics closer to the exam will help make sure they are fresh in students' minds.

The chart below shows the units and the time suggested for each unit. The number of class periods is based on a typical 45-minute class. If your school is on a form of block schedule or other non-typical schedule, you will need to adjust the pacing to fit your class needs.

| TOPICS | PACING | 5 STEPS TO A 5 |
| --- | --- | --- |
| **Unit 1:** Scientific Foundations of Psychology (10–14%) | 15–16 Class Periods | Chapter 5, pp. 53–76 |
| **Unit 2:** Biological Bases of Behavior (8–10%) | 14–15 Class Periods | Chapter 6, pp. 77–105 |
| **Unit 3:** Sensation and Perception (6–8%) | 12–13 Class Periods | Chapter 7, pp. 106–124 |
| **Unit 4:** Learning (7–9%) | 12–13 Class Periods | Chapter 8, pp. 125–139 |
| **Unit 5:** Cognition (13–17%) | 20–21 Class Periods | Chapter 9, pp. 140–170 |
| **Unit 6:** Developmental Psychology (7–9%) | 12–13 Class Periods | Chapter 10, pp. 171–191 |
| **Unit 7:** Motivation, Emotion, and Personality (11–15%) | 14–15 Class Periods | Chapter 11, pp. 192–225 |
| **Unit 8:** Clinical Psychology (12–16%) | 16–17 Class Periods | Chapter 12, pp. 226–253 |
| **Unit 9:** Social Psychology (8–10%) | 14–15 Class Periods | Chapter 13, pp. 254–267 |

As you plan your year, try to leave a day for review for each unit, two days at the end of fall semester, and a full week, if possible, in the spring semester. I'm always surprised with how much students don't remember from just a few months prior.

## STEP 2

# Hold an Interesting Class Every Day

AP psychology students should love coming to your class; as I like to say, "Psych is everywhere." There are countless opportunities for students to make connections to their own lives and the world around them, it's incredible to see this awakening in students.

I follow a similar schedule daily with different activities that keep the class interesting, and students engaged. It is also extremely important to build relationships with your students. I find that by spending just a few minutes each day checking in about the latest after-school activities, jobs, and current sports, students feel much more comfortable in the classroom environment, which adds tremendously to their "buy in" of doing the work and participating.

▶ **Opener.** I always have a funny cartoon, article, or recent event that connects to the topic(s) we will be examining that day.

▶ **Lecture/notes.** I upload my notes (I use PowerPoint) to the students' learning management system (we use Schoology) and I print out unit packets for each student. Some students prefer to take their notes electronically and this system enables them to take notes directly on their tablet or electronic device. This saves hours of time, because I can quickly address the important or often misunderstood sections of the notes, skipping over the things they can study and learn on their own. I do my best not to lecture for more than 20 minutes per day; often I only lecture for 15 minutes.

▶ **Activity/lab/video.** So far, we have used about 25 minutes, so I still have 30 minutes of time to do something that involves movement, discussion, connections, and engagement. Hands-on labs, group activities, a movie/ documentary, etc., all fall into this category. Some units may have more group activities and movies. For other units, there are so many lab ideas that you will need to pick and choose.

▶ **Homework.** In my AP psychology course, I have the expectation that the course will model that of a college experience. I also like to give students the ownership, flexibility, and accountability of determining the "right amount" of homework for them on a daily/ weekly basis. In doing this, I've created a system called "RON"; we actually pretend this is a person, have a poster of him in class, and talk about him as if he's a buddy. In actuality, RON just stands for Reading, Outlining, and Notecards. I provide a suggested pacing guide for each unit in terms of how much a student should be reading and completing of their notecards on average, but it also gives them the flexibility to do more work on the weekend or a night that don't have as many extracurricular activities. There are some students that this is "too much" ownership on their part, and they want more structure

as they tend to procrastinate. For these students, the pacing guide is not optional, but something I check on Monday, Wednesday, and Friday each week.

If you have a classroom set of the *5 Steps to a 5 AP Psychology*, you can assign the students the homework of reading a few pages of the book that correlates to the lesson you are teaching next. The review questions at the end of each chapter are an excellent means of formative assessment and also make for a fun review game. I like to divide the class into teams, and they get one question at a time before they get their next clue (i.e., question); this makes it a competition between the groups. The book is also available online with flashcards, games, and other extras; check the back cover of this book for instructions for accessing the online edition.

The labs, classroom activities, and videos/ documentaries that you decide to use in your course will depend on your interests, school budget, class composition, culture, and norms. However, there are some activities that are used in many AP psychology classrooms, and these are listed below by unit. A quick Google search will usually find all of these activities (search for videos by title). In addition, you might consider joining a Facebook page that is specifically for AP psychology teachers. If you go to Facebook and search "AP Psychology Teachers group," you will find it immediately. This group, which has over 7,000 members, has wonderful ideas—way more than you could possibly do in a year. Here are some of my favorite classroom activities.

# Supplemental Resource to Enhance Instruction

| **Unit 1:** Scientific Foundations of Psychology | ▶ Monty Hall Problem. https://www.youtube.com/watch?v=cXqDIFUB7YU<br>▶ Correlation: Joy of Stats. https://www.youtube.com/watch?v=6RzDMEW5omc<br>▶ Skittles (or M&Ms) in teaching statistics.<br>▶ Are you ready for some football? (Measures of Variability)<br>▶ Ted Talks on Statistics. https://www.ted.com/topics/statistics |
|---|---|
| **Unit 2:** Biological Bases of Behavior | ▶ Candy Neuron/Chalk Neurons<br>▶ Orange Brain Surgery<br>▶ Mouse Party<br>▶ Netflix: *An Unnatural Selection*<br>▶ Phineas Gage Song/Video/Article<br>▶ Pinky and the Brain Video<br>▶ Severed Corpus Callosum: David Gazzaniga's research |
| **Unit 3:** Sensation and Perception | ▶ Video: *The Boy Who Could See Without Eyes*<br>▶ Movie: *The Sound of Fury*<br>▶ 3D Human Ear. http://www.youtube.com/watch?v=0jyxhozq89g<br>▶ Awareness Test: Moonwalking Bear. http://www.youtube.com/watch?v=oSQJP40PcGI<br>▶ Brain Games: Pay Attention. https://www.dailymotion.com/video/x1zwwx4<br>▶ Change Blindness: Whodoneit? http://www.youtube.com/watch?v=ubNF9QNEQLA<br>▶ Rubber Hand Illusion. http://www.youtube.com/watch?v=sxwn1w7MJvk<br>▶ Brain Games: Pay Attention. https://www.youtube.com/watch?v=jBApdNXk5IA&list=PLrUdmzqCBEbJA6NrY_FGTAGWanEfZ7dvi |
| **Unit 4:** Learning | ▶ What happened to Little Albert? https://www.youtube.com/watch?v=KJnJ1Q8PAJk<br>▶ *The Office: Altoids*. https://www.youtube.com/watch?v=PBb1CH18Smg<br>▶ Ivan Pavlov. https://www.youtube.com/watch?v=hhqumfpxuzI<br>▶ John Watson: Baby Albert Experiments. https://www.youtube.com/watch?v=FMnhyGozLyE<br>▶ Children See, Children Do. https://www.youtube.com/watch?v=KHi2dxSf9hw<br>▶ Bandura and Bobo Doll. https://www.youtube.com/watch?v=6lYsmt9qUVI |
| **Unit 5:** Cognition | ▶ Eyewitness Testimony. http://www.psmag.com/footnotes/see-eyewitness-testimony-fail-eyes-90728/#.VBzYmnaqNUo.twitter<br>▶ Ted Talk: Elizabeth Loftus. https://www.ted.com/talks/elizabeth_loftus_how_reliable_is_your_memory?language=en<br>▶ 60 Minutes: *Elizabeth Loftus*. https://www.youtube.com/watch?v=XcywPdORySA<br>▶ 60 Minutes: *Superior Autobiographical Memory, Part 1*. https://www.youtube.com/watch?v=oHeEQ85m79I<br>▶ 60 Minutes: *Superior Autobiographical Memory, Part 2*. https://www.youtube.com/watch?v=1th1fVIc8Vo<br>▶ Clive Wearing: The Man with a 30 Second Memory. https://www.youtube.com/watch?v=WmzU47i2xgw<br>▶ Gobbledygook. https://www.youtube.com/watch?v=fbgnieG9Z4g<br>▶ Availability Heuristic. https://kenthendricks.com/availability-heuristic/<br>▶ Kids teach Alan Alda and Steven Pinker How to Talk. https://www.youtube.com/watch?v=IhVZovbL0Zs<br>▶ GENIE. https://www.youtube.com/watch?v=VjZolHCrC8E&list=PL_EdRI4QWW3MgKkh65Ax8C__xN_n19hts |

*(continued)*

| Unit 6: Developmental Psychology | ▶ Newborn Reflexes. https://www.youtube.com/watch?v=0vrdkzOnGgo<br>▶ Piaget and Conservation. https://www.youtube.com/watch?v=QxUxgPwpfgk<br>▶ Piaget and Object Permanence. http://www.youtube.com/watch?v=ue8y-JVhjS0&feature=related<br>▶ Piaget and Egocentrism. https://www.youtube.com/watch?v=RDJ0qJTLohM<br>▶ Piaget and Concrete Operational Thought. https://www.youtube.com/watch?v=gA04ew6Oi9M<br>▶ Piaget and Formal Thought. http://www.youtube.com/watch?v=zjJdcXA1KH8&feature=related<br>▶ TED talk (from 2:17–5 min) Conception to Birth. https://www.youtube.com/watch?v=fKyljukBE70<br>▶ Harlow. https://www.youtube.com/watch?v=OrNBEhzjg8I<br>▶ Baby Training-Myrtle McGraw. https://www.youtube.com/watch?v=z0feuLSe4xE&list=PLiU8GDF2aDLZgqptTPeqchCivrqKD_bsr<br>▶ Sophie Can Walk (make sure to get *edited* version). https://www.youtube.com/watch?v=Nm42kzGFd6g |
| --- | --- |
| Unit 7: Motivation, Emotion, and Personality | ▶ I Survived: Alive (watch first 3 minutes and then cue to 25:40 for an additional 9+ minutes). https://www.youtube.com/watch?v=jlGepBHFe5M<br>▶ Eating Disorders from the Inside Out (TEDxTalk) with Dr. Laura Hill. https://www.youtube.com/watch?v=UEysOExcwrE&t=2s<br>▶ Hypothalamic Obesity. https://www.youtube.com/watch?v=AVVjVKQB18I&t=4s<br>▶ Dan Gilbert TED talk: The Surprising Science of Happiness. https://www.ted.com/talks/dan_gilbert_the_surprising_science_of_happiness?language=en<br>▶ Martin Seligman TED talk: The New Era of Positive Psychology. https://www.ted.com/talks/martin_seligman_the_new_era_of_positive_psychology?language=en<br>▶ Daniel Goleman TED talk: Why aren't we more compassionate? https://www.ted.com/talks/daniel_goleman_why_aren_t_we_more_compassionate?language=en<br>▶ What is Psychoanalysis? From the Institute of Psychoanalysis, a short, animated comic on what psychoanalysis is. http://www.youtube.com/watch?v=uM2FGc0wDg8&feature=related<br>▶ Freud: Under Analysis. Nova (entire video is online—47 minutes). https://www.youtube.com/watch?v=3qQJdam4jiE<br>▶ Freud's Id/Ego/Superego: Emperor's New Groove clip of Krunk's Dilemma. http://www.youtube.com/watch?v=VnMGCUH-ILY<br>▶ The Big Personality Test, BBC (How personality develops in childhood.) https://www.youtube.com/watch?v=7OuuvICk89Q<br>▶ Myers-Briggs. https://www.youtube.com/watch?v=hmZn6pWbSG4<br>▶ Defense Mechanisms. http://youtu.be/FnRBAU6Yg2A<br>▶ Freudian Slip. http://www.youtube.com/watch?v=ARCEXnesa7g |
| Unit 8: Clinical Psychology | ▶ Young & Schizophrenic.<br>▶ Gerald the Schizophrenic. http://www.youtube.com/watch?v=gGnI8dqEoPQ<br>▶ Overcoming Schizophrenia and the Real John Nash (A Beautiful Mind).<br>▶ Hallucinations. |

|  |  |
|---|---|
|  | ▶ Disassociate Amnesia & Repressed Childhood Memories. |
|  | ▶ Dissociative Fugue MSNBC clip. |
|  | ▶ OCD and Rituals. |
|  | ▶ Mania (Bipolar Disorder). |
|  | ▶ Bipolar Disorder (mania). |
|  | ▶ *The Sopranos*. Tony experiences transference when he tells Dr. Melfi he loves her. (Preview & stop at 2:00 or bleep the f*** word.) http://www.youtube.com/watch?v=qbS2N88paTs |
|  | ▶ Therapeutic Effects of Antipsychotics. |
|  | ▶ Undesired Effects of Antipsychotics. |
|  | ▶ Tardive Dyskinesia. http://www.youtube.com/watch?v=W_3bbpFjI68 |
|  | ▶ Aversion Therapy. (A very funny spoof of aversion therapy and fast food eating.) |
|  | ▶ *Big Bang Theory* & Psychoanalysis (Leonard psychoanalyzes Sheldon). http://www.youtube.com/watch?v=uZq_U2hbnvs&feature=related |
|  | ▶ Albert Ellis. http://www.youtube.com/watch?v=EHK9zxk0Beo |
|  | ▶ Albert Ellis and Gloria. https://www.youtube.com/watch?v=tcq4RMzSyng |
|  | ▶ Virtual Reality Therapy & Treating Panic Disorder. http://www.youtube.com/watch?v=CQgKEp_NhHk |
|  | ▶ Hypnosis For Hoarding. https://www.youtube.com/watch?v=tjA-J_Af7X4 |
| **Unit 9:** Social Psychology | ▶ Highwayman/Wife Scenario; Just World Hypotheses |
|  | ▶ The Social Dilemma, Netflix |
|  | ▶ Latane and Darley bystander effect video |
|  | ▶ Milgram's Shock Experiment |
|  | ▶ The Stanford Prison Experiment (have ½ class watch the original with Zimbardo and the other half watch the more recent version for an interesting discussion). Make sure to follow up with critiques of the study. |
|  | ▶ 38 Witnesses: ID Channel (watch first 10 minutes and last 15). |
|  | ▶ Bystander Effect. (More current examples from NYC) https://www.youtube.com/watch?v=g-WvaRJdAA0 |
|  | ▶ *History Channel* clip: Bystander Effect (6:43) |
|  | ▶ *The Office: Diversity Day*. |
|  | ▶ *The Office: Conflict*. |

*5 Steps to a 5 AP Psychology: Elite Edition*

The Elite Edition provides additional questions that can be used in your class. It contains 180 activities and questions that require five minutes a day. While they are primarily intended to be used by students studying for the test, you can use these as daily warm-ups in your course. To do this, you will need the table below that organizes these questions and activities by unit since they do not follow the course in chronological order.

| UNIT | QUESTIONS/ACTIVITIES IN THE ELITE EDITION |
|---|---|
| **Unit 1:** Scientific Foundations of Psychology | Days 1–15 (pp. 329–343) |
| **Unit 2:** Biological Bases of Behavior | Days 16–30 (pp. 344–358); Days 45–56 (pp. 373–384) |
| **Unit 3:** Sensation and Perception | Days 31–44 (pp. 359–372) |
| **Unit 4:** Learning | Days 57–73 (pp. 385–401) |
| **Unit 5:** Cognition | Days 74–93 (pp. 402–421); Days 145–153 (pp. 473–481) |
| **Unit 6:** Developmental Psychology | Days 108–122 (pp. 436–450) |
| **Unit 7:** Motivation, Emotion, and Personality | Days 94–107 (pp. 422–435); Days 123–144 (pp. 451–472) |
| **Unit 8:** Clinical Psychology | Days 154–172 (pp. 482–500) |
| **Unit 9:** Social Psychology | Days 173–180 (pp. 501–508) |

# STEP 3

# Evaluate Your Students' Progress

I give students between 35–55 multiple-choice questions for each unit during the fall term. I recommend that you incorporate released AP questions from the College Board (found on AP Classroom) on your unit exams. You can also add additional questions from your textbook, from *5 Steps to a 5 AP Psychology,* or those you create yourself. However, there is no better resource than the people that write the test and there are over a thousand questions on AP classroom for you to use.

It's ideal to include a FRQ on each of your unit exams. However, I do not start having the students practice FRQs until the spring term as most FRQ questions draw from several different units. You can always adjust the FRQs during the fall term and add/delete concepts accordingly. Getting the students to practice responding to an open-ended question in the exam format is a great way to help them on the AP exam. Remember, there are two FRQs on the AP exam and the FRQs count for a third of each student's score.

I use the acronym PEST in teaching the "how to" in writing an AP psychology essay.

| P | Paragraph format | Students need to write in complete sentences, but they DO NOT need an introduction or transitional statements. |
|---|---|---|
| E | Examples | Always use examples with your application as these are where the points are earned. |
| S | Stay in ORDER (of the question) | This allows the AP reader to more easily follow your train of thought in case you leave out the name of the concept you are describing. |
| T | Time | You only have 50 minutes to answer both FRQs; make sure to budget your time accordingly so you don't miss out on easy points in the second question. |

You can use a peer review process for grading or have students grade their own FRQs in class. This not only saves you time but is extremely effective in helping students understand how points are awarded on the actual AP exam. My students do not feel comfortable with other students grading their work, so I usually have them grade their own work, giving points where they believe they scored points and then I go through them afterwards for accuracy. I often allow students to re-do them for full credit as this encourages the learning process.

When we first begin writing FRQs, I allow students to work in groups to ease the pressure. I then separate an FRQ into its various parts (usually 8–10) and have students move between stations answering the different parts. They have to agree with or edit what the person before them wrote. This allows for movement in the classroom and minimizes the risk involved with writing a FRQ.

I have students to do test corrections for *every* multiple-choice test using our metacognitive process. Test corrections are an important part of the learning process. I use a grading program called Illuminate that allows me to scan with the camera on my computer each student's test for immediate feedback (as we know this is the most powerful). I then print out factor analysis sheets for each test using this program so students can see where their strengths are and the areas they need to work on. For example, on the cognition test, it would break the questions into groups so students would know how they did on the memory portion, compared to the problem-solving types of questions, as opposed to the language questions. Students can begin working on these immediately after the unit test.

I give them around 25 minutes of class time and if they have remaining work to do, they need to come in during the allocated "help time" at our school or at lunch. I have students keep a folder in my class where all of their tests are stored. Tests are NOT allowed to leave the room, but this gives students ownership over the assessment process. They know specific areas they need to work on and use these folders as a guide in studying for the final, midterm, and AP exam. Below is an example of the worksheet that the students need to complete. (Extend the form so that it fills the page, but keep plenty of room in the vertical spacing for complex answers.)

# Metacognition: Thinking About Thinking

## Analyzing the Results of Your Test

### Unit (Test Name) _____

Instructions: For each question you missed on the unit exam, complete the grid below.

| QUESTION # | CONCEPT<br>Explain the concept in detail so that when you look at your explanation when you study again, it clearly explains the concept involved in this question. | WHY I MISSED THIS QUESTION | WHAT I KNOW NOW |
|---|---|---|---|
| | | | |
| | | | |
| | | | |

I use a total points system in my course in which tests account for approximately 40% of their grade; homework is an additional 40% (this is the "RON" I was referring to earlier), and the remaining 10% comes from writing.

## STEP 4

# Get Students Ready to Take the AP Exam

If you have left two weeks to review, you are in great shape! I start the review process by giving a diagnostic test. This could come from AP classroom or from this book (Chapter 3) as long as students haven't already looked at the answers. You will want to have the students do a factor analysis of their results. If you have a grading program like Illuminate, you can enter these standards and it will give each student a slip with this already done. However, before I had this program, we just used a simple system of corresponding the questions to the unit. The diagnostic test in *5 Steps to a 5* is a great example of this (see pages 34–35). This process allows students to hone in on the areas that need the most attention.

Each session I focus on a particular unit. If you do not have 9 days (one for each unit) to review, you can start the review process three weeks before the AP exam and hold these sessions virtually after school or on the weekends. You can hold three per week and students can attend the ones in the areas in which they need the most help. I survey my students to see if there's a time that's more convenient for them (usually it's Saturday or Sunday mornings). If the students prefer, you can hold the review sessions virtually.

All of my review resources are posted on a Schoology page solely focused on the AP exam. I post practice FRQ questions that students can submit, all the information from each unit we covered in the course, and a discussion board where students can help one another.

**Unit 1: Scientific Foundations of Psychology**
15 minutes: Research-based FRQ as a class

**Unit 2: Biological Bases of Behavior**
15 minutes: Multi-unit FRQ as a class

**Unit 3: Sensation and Perception**
15 minutes: Research-based FRQ as a class

**Unit 4: Learning**
15 minutes: Multi-unit FRQ as a class

**Unit 5: Cognition**
15 minutes: Research-based FRQ as a class

**Unit 6: Developmental Psychology**
15 minutes: Multi-unit FRQ as a class

**Unit 7: Motivation, Emotion, and Personality**
15 minutes: Research-based FRQ as a class

**Unit 8: Clinical Psychology**
15 minutes: Multi-unit FRQ as a class

**Unit 9: Social Psychology**
15 minutes: Research-based FRQ as a class

We spend the remaining 30 minutes working in two stations. Here are some of the choices that students have:

▶ **Station 1: Review a Chapter in *5 Steps to a 5 AP Psychology*.** If you have multiple copies of this book, students can use it to review. This is especially important if the diagnostic test showed there was a chapter that they just didn't get the first time. The text in this book explains the subject, key terms are identified and defined, and review questions check the student's understanding.

▶ **Station 2: Make Your Own Review Card.** You know those laminated poster-like cards they sell to students to review? They can make their own now that they know what topics they need to study. Then they walk away with personalized study card just for them. I provide the students with a blank file folder and a variety of markers.

▸ **Station 3: Similar but Different.** I have a list of some of the most confusing pairs in psychology (see below) and students need to explain to their partner how this concept relates but also what makes them different.

▸ **Station 4: Kahoot.** There are so many Kahoots that pertain to each unit in AP psychology. I post options for them on our Schoology page and students can work on the areas they need the most help with.

▸ **Station 5: FRQs.** I have every single released FRQ printed on one side with the scoring rubrics on the other side (you can get this from the AP classroom). The students can pair up or work on their own. They analyze the question and think about or actually compose a response, and then check their work with the scoring guideline to see if they would have received each point.

▸ **Station 6: Take a Practice Exam.** You can have a station where students can practice taking the test using the released tests found in the AP classroom. If you have multiple copies of *5 Steps to a 5 AP Psychology*, students can take the two full-length practice exams found at the end of the book and score themselves. Taking the diagnostic test found in Chapter 3 of this book is especially useful for the students if you have done so already.

▸ **Station 7: AP Classroom Videos.** At this station, I have a computer or iPad and the students can simply log in to their own AP classroom and watch the videos that correspond to the units and topics they found from their diagnostic exam that they needed the most help on. You can set this station up with headphones, so they don't disturb others.

▸ **Station 8: Small-Group Study Sessions with the Teacher.** This gives me the opportunity to work with a small group of students throughout the two weeks of review, giving specialized feedback in areas they have the most questions and work on improving their writing.

Some students are going to take advantage of *all* the review opportunities you provide; others may only do what is offered in class. My best piece of advice is trying as many ways of getting kids to think about psychology outside of your classroom. For example, I will tweet out funny examples of psych in my life for 30 days prior to the AP exam. I'll send remind texts that are encouraging, yet deliberate in motivating students. I bring lots of food to the review sessions and tweet the pictures prior (food usually works the best). Get them excited about taking the test. I always say, "This is your opportunity to show what you know" (like that framing?).

## STEP 5

# Become a Better Teacher Every Year

Becoming a better AP psychology teacher involves a growth mindset. This mindset will allow you to seek out better instructional strategies and ideas to improve your AP classroom each and every year. The best AP teachers are not ones who believe they have "figured it out," but ones who look to improve through self-reflection and growth. Teaching AP psychology can seem overwhelming the first year (or few years), but each year gets easier and better as you see what lessons students really respond to and where there are areas for improvement.

How do you judge success? We all have a different population of students, different schedules, and varying resources. You can do this in a quantitative manner if you'd like by seeing if there's a correlation between their grades in your class (on your tests) and their AP score. You can measure their growth throughout the year on FRQs and MCs, but I prefer to look at it more qualitatively. Are students enjoying the learning process and getting the skills and information they need to be successful in a college-level psychology course?

The College Board, via their Instructional Planning Report, will give you plenty of quantitative data after the exam that you can use in preparing for the following year of instruction. Look for trends such as a unit or topic that students excelled in and areas that needed improvement. How did they do on the MC portion compared to the FRQ portion? Are you spending enough time on the FRQs?

In addition, giving students an "exit survey" of sorts will also gather useful information. This is an example from my Google survey form I use:

---

**Name:**

Short answer text

---

**Please explain 3 concepts and/or examples from units that you enjoyed, learned from, and can use:**

Long answer text

---

**Please explain 1-3 areas that you would have improved or topics you would have liked to explore further:**

Long answer text

---

**Any other feedback is greatly appreciated:**

Long answer text

---

Another phenomenal resource is the AP Summer Institute, where you will have the opportunity to lesson plan, harvest ideas, and network. Once you have taught AP for three years, you can apply online through the College Board's website to be an AP reader. This is the best professional development I have experienced as an educator. It is from the AP reading that I have created my own professional learning community made up of teachers from around the United States; these fellow educators have enriched my teaching in countless ways.